THE
REMARKABLE
SOUL OF A
Woman

DIETER F. UCHTDORF

DESERET
BOOK

Salt Lake City, Utah

This booklet is an adaptation of an address delivered at the general Relief Society meeting on September 27, 2008.

Visit us at DeseretBook.com

Library of Congress Cataloging-in-Publication Data
Uchtdorf, Dieter F.
  The remarkable soul of a woman / Dieter F. Uchtdorf.
     p. cm.
  Adaptation of an address delivered at the general Relief Society meeting of
The Church of Jesus Christ of Latter-day Saints on September 27, 2008.
  ISBN 978-1-60641-244-2 (hardbound : alk. paper)
  1. Women—Religious aspects—The Church of Jesus Christ of Latter-day Saints.
  2. Mormon women. I. Title.
  BX8641.U24 2010
  248.8′430882893—dc22   2010001940

Printed in the United States of America
Worzalla Publishing Co., Stevens Point, WI
10   9   8   7   6   5   4   3   2   1

THEREFORE TREASURE UP
THESE WORDS IN THY HEART.
BE FAITHFUL AND DILIGENT IN
KEEPING THE COMMANDMENTS
OF GOD, AND I WILL ENCIRCLE
THEE IN THE ARMS OF MY LOVE.

—D&C 6:20

THE REMARKABLE
SOUL OF A WOMAN

I have thought about the many women who have shaped my life: my wonderful wife, Harriet; my mother; my mother-in-law; my sister; my daughter; my daughter-in-law; and many friends. All my life I have been surrounded by women who inspired, taught, and encouraged me. I am who I am today in large part because of these singular women. Each time I meet with the sisters of the Church, I sense that I am in the midst of similar remarkable souls. I am grateful for your talents, compassion, and service. Most of all, I am grateful for who you

Most of all, I am
grateful for who you are:
a treasured daughter of
our Heavenly Father
with infinite worth.

are: a treasured daughter of our Heavenly Father with infinite worth.

I'm sure it comes as no surprise, but the differences between men and women can often be quite striking—physically and mentally, as well as emotionally. One of the best ways I can think of to illustrate this is in the way my wife and I cook a meal.

When Harriet prepares a meal, it's a masterpiece. Her cuisine is as wide-ranging as the world, and she frequently prepares dishes from countries we have visited. The presentation of the food is awe inspiring. In fact, it often looks so beautiful that it seems a crime to eat it. It's as much a feast for the eyes as it is for the sense of taste.

But sure enough, no matter how perfect everything is, looks, and tastes, Harriet will apologize for something she thinks is imperfect. "I'm afraid I used a touch too much ginger," she will say, or, "Next time, I think it would be better if I used a little more curry and one additional bay leaf."

Let me contrast that with the way I cook. For the purpose of this talk, I asked Harriet to tell me what I cook best.

Her answer: fried eggs.

Sunny-side up.

But that isn't all. I have a specialty dish called *Knusperchen.* The name may sound like a delicacy you might find at an exclusive restaurant. Let me share with you how to make it. You cut French bread into small slices and toast them twice.

That is the recipe!

So, between fried eggs, even when they are greasy, and *Knusperchen,* even when they are burned, when I cook, I feel pretty heroic.

Perhaps this contrast between my wife and me is a slight exaggeration, but it illustrates something that may extend beyond preparing meals.

To me it appears that our splendid sisters sometimes undervalue their abilities—they focus on what is lacking or imperfect rather than what has been accomplished and who they really are.

Perhaps you recognize this trait in someone you know really well.

The good news is that this also points to an admirable quality: the innate desire to please the Lord to the best of your ability. Unfortunately, it can also lead to frustration, exhaustion, and unhappiness.

To All Who
Are Weary

I would like to address those who have ever felt inadequate, discouraged, or weary—in short, I would like to address all of us.

I also pray that the Holy Ghost will amplify my words and bestow upon them additional meaning, insight, and inspiration.

We know that sometimes it can be difficult to keep our heads above water. In fact, in our world of change, challenges, and checklists, sometimes it can seem nearly impossible to avoid feeling overwhelmed by emotions of suffering and sorrow.

I am not suggesting that we can simply flip a switch and stop the negative feelings that distress us. This isn't a pep talk or an attempt to encourage those sinking in quicksand to imagine instead that they are relaxing on a beach. I recognize that in all of our lives there are real concerns. I know there are hearts that harbor deep sorrows. Others wrestle with fears that trouble the soul. For some, loneliness is their secret trial.

These things are not insignificant.

However, I would like to share two principles that may help us find a path to peace, hope, and joy—even during times of trial and distress. I want to address God's happiness and how each one of us can taste of it in spite of the burdens that beset us.

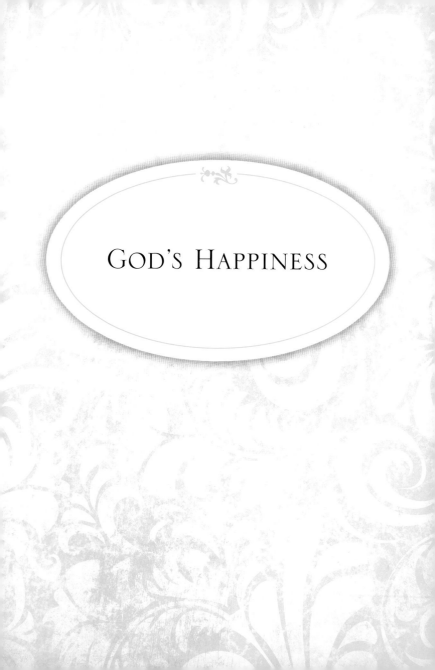

GOD'S HAPPINESS

L et me first pose a question: What do you suppose is the greatest kind of happiness possible? For me, the answer to this question is, God's happiness.

This leads to another question: What is our Heavenly Father's happiness?

This may be impossible to answer because His ways are not our ways. "For as the heavens are higher than the earth, so are [God's] ways higher than [our] ways, and [His] thoughts [higher] than [our] thoughts."[1]

Though we cannot understand "the meaning of all things," we do "know that [God] loveth his children."

Though we cannot understand "the meaning of all things," we do "know that [God] loveth his children"[2] because He has said, "Behold, this is my work and my glory—to bring to pass the immortality and eternal life of man."[3]

Heavenly Father is able to accomplish these two great goals—the immortality and eternal life of man—because He is a God of creation and compassion. Creating and being compassionate are two objectives that contribute to our Heavenly Father's perfect happiness. Creating and being compassionate are two activities that we as His spirit children can and should emulate.

THE WORK
OF CREATION

The desire to create is one of the deepest yearnings of the human soul. No matter our talents, education, backgrounds, or abilities, we each have an inherent wish to create something that did not exist before.

Everyone can create. We don't need money, position, or influence in order to create something of substance or beauty.

Creation brings deep satisfaction and fulfillment. We develop ourselves and others when we take unorganized matter into our hands and mold it into

WE EACH HAVE AN
INHERENT WISH TO CREATE
SOMETHING THAT DID NOT
EXIST BEFORE.

something of beauty—and I am *not* talking about the process of cleaning the rooms of your teenage children.

You might say, "I'm not the creative type. When I sing, I'm always half a tone above or below the note. I cannot draw a line without a ruler. And the only practical use for my homemade bread is as a paperweight or doorstop."

If that is how you feel, think again, and remember that you are a spirit daughter of the most creative Being in the universe. Isn't it remarkable to think that your very spirit is fashioned by an endlessly creative and eternally compassionate God? Think about it—your spirit body is a masterpiece, created with a beauty, function, and capacity beyond imagination.

But to what end were you created? You were created with the express purpose and potential of experiencing a fulness of joy.[4] Your birthright—and the purpose of your great voyage on this earth—is to seek and experience eternal happiness. One of the ways you find this is by creating things.

If you are a mother, you participate with God in His work of creation—not only by providing physical bodies for your children but also by teaching and nurturing them. If you are not a mother now, the creative talents you develop will prepare you for that day, in this life or the next.

You may think you don't have talents, but that is a false assumption, for we all have talents and gifts, every one of us.[5] The bounds of creativity extend far beyond the limits of a canvas or a sheet of paper and do not require a brush, a pen, or the keys of a piano. Creation means bringing into existence something that did not exist before—colorful gardens, harmonious homes, family memories, flowing laughter.

What you create doesn't have to be perfect. So what if the eggs are greasy or the toast is burned? Don't let fear of failure discourage you. Don't let the voice of critics paralyze you—whether that voice comes from the outside or the inside.

If you still feel incapable of creating, start small. Try to see how many smiles you can create; write a letter of appreciation; learn a new skill; identify a space and beautify it.

Nearly a century and a half ago, President Brigham Young spoke to the Saints of his day. "There is a great work for the Saints to do," he said. "Progress, and improve upon and make beautiful everything around you. Cultivate the earth, and cultivate your minds. Build cities, adorn your habitations, make gardens, orchards, and vineyards, and render the earth so pleasant that when you look upon your labors you may do so with pleasure, and that angels may delight to come and visit your beautiful locations. In the meantime continually seek to adorn your minds with all the graces of the Spirit of Christ."[6] The more you trust and rely upon the Spirit, the greater your capacity to create. That is your opportunity in this life and your destiny in the life to come. Trust and rely on the

Spirit. As you take the normal opportunities of your daily life and create something of beauty and helpfulness, you improve not only the world around you but also the world within you.

BEING
COMPASSIONATE

WHEN YOU REACH OUT
TO BLESS THE LIVES OF
OTHERS, YOUR LIFE IS
BLESSED AS WELL.

eing compassionate is another great work of our Heavenly Father and a fundamental characteristic of who we are as a people. We are commanded to "succor the weak, lift up the hands which hang down, and strengthen the feeble knees."[7] Disciples of Christ throughout all ages of the world have been distinguished by their compassion. Those who follow the Savior "mourn with those that mourn . . . and comfort those that stand in need of comfort."[8] When you reach out to bless the lives of others, your life is blessed as well. Service

and sacrifice open the windows of heaven, allowing choice blessings to descend upon you. Surely your beloved Heavenly Father smiles upon those who care for the least of His children.

As you lift others, you rise a little higher yourself. President Spencer W. Kimball taught, "The more we serve our fellowmen in appropriate ways, the more substance there is to our souls."[9]

President Gordon B. Hinckley believed in the healing power of service. After the death of his wife, he provided a great example to the Church in the way he immersed himself in work and in serving others. It is told that President Hinckley remarked to one woman who had recently lost her husband, "Work will cure your grief. Serve others."

These are profound words. As you lose yourself in the service of others, you discover your own life and your own happiness.

President Lorenzo Snow expressed a similar thought: "When you find yourselves a little gloomy, look around you and find somebody that is in a worse plight than yourself; go to him and find out what the trouble is, then try to remove it with the wisdom which the Lord bestows upon you; and the first thing you know, your gloom is gone, you feel light, the Spirit of the Lord is upon you, and everything seems illuminated."[10]

In today's world of pop psychology, junk TV, and feel-good self-help manuals, this advice may seem counterintuitive. We are sometimes told that the answer to our ills is to look inward, to indulge ourselves, to spend first and pay later, and to satisfy our own desires even at the expense of those around us. While there are times when it is prudent to look first to our own needs, in the long run it doesn't lead to lasting happiness.

An Instrument in the Hands of the Lord

OFTEN SMALL ACTS OF
SERVICE ARE ALL THAT
IS REQUIRED TO LIFT
AND BLESS ANOTHER.

I believe that the women of the Church, regardless of age or family status, understand and apply best the words of James Barrie, the author of *Peter Pan:* "Those who bring sunshine to the lives of others cannot keep it from themselves."[11] Often I have witnessed quiet acts of kindness and compassion by noble women who extended themselves in unselfish charity. My heart swells when I hear stories of the sisters of the Church and how they rush to the aid of those in need.

There are those in the Church—both men and

women—who wonder how they can contribute to the kingdom. Sometimes women who are single, divorced, or widowed wonder if there is a place for them. *Every* sister in the Church is of critical importance—not only to our Heavenly Father but to the building of the kingdom of God as well. There is a great work to do.

In the 2007 general Relief Society meeting, President Monson taught that "you are . . . surrounded by opportunities for service. . . . Often small acts of service are all that is required to lift and bless another."[12] Look around you. There at sacrament meeting is a young mother with several children—offer to sit with her and help. There in your neighborhood is a young person who seems discouraged—tell him you enjoy being in his presence, tell her that you feel her goodness. True words of encouragement require only a loving and caring heart but may have an eternal impact on the lives of those around you.

As a sister in the gospel, you render compassionate service to others for reasons that supersede desires for personal benefits. In this you emulate the Savior, who, though a King, did not seek position, nor was He concerned about whether others noticed Him. He did not bother to compete with others. His thoughts were always tuned to help others. He taught, healed, conversed, and listened to others. He knew that greatness had little to do with outward signs of prosperity or position. He taught and lived by this doctrine: "He that is greatest among you shall be your servant."[13]

In the end, the number of prayers we say may contribute to our happiness, but the number of prayers we answer may be of even greater importance. Let us open our eyes and see the heavy hearts, notice the loneliness and despair; let us feel the silent prayers of others around us; and let us be an instrument in the hands of the Lord to answer those prayers.

CONCLUSION

I have a simple faith. I believe that as you are faithful and diligent in keeping the commandments of God, as you draw closer to Him in faith, hope, and charity, things will work together for your good.[14] I believe that as you immerse yourself in the work of our Father—as you create beauty and as you are compassionate to others—God will encircle you in the arms of His love.[15] Discouragement, inadequacy, and weariness will give way to a life of meaning, grace, and fulfillment.

As a spirit daughter of our Heavenly Father, happiness is your heritage.

You are a choice daughter of our Heavenly Father, and through the things you create and by your compassionate service, you are a great power for good. You will make the world a better place. Lift up your chin; walk tall. God loves you. We love and admire you.

SEARCH DILIGENTLY, PRAY
ALWAYS, AND BE BELIEVING,
AND ALL THINGS SHALL WORK
TOGETHER FOR YOUR GOOD, IF YE
WALK UPRIGHTLY AND REMEMBER
THE COVENANT WHEREWITH
YE HAVE COVENANTED ONE
WITH ANOTHER.

—D&C 90:24

NOTES

1. Isaiah 55:9.

2. 1 Nephi 11:17.

3. Moses 1:39.

4. See 2 Nephi 2:25.

5. See D&C 46:11–12.

6. Brigham Young, *Deseret News,* August 8, 1860, 177.

7. D&C 81:5.

8. Mosiah 18:9.

9. *The Teachings of Spencer W. Kimball,* ed. Edward L. Kimball (Salt Lake City: Bookcraft, 1982), 254.

10. Lorenzo Snow, in Conference Report, April 1899, 2–3.

11. J. M. Barrie, *A Window in Thrums* (New York City: Charles Scribner's Sons, 1917), 137.

12. Thomas S. Monson, "Three Goals to Guide You," *Liahona* and *Ensign,* November 2007, 120.

13. Matthew 23:11.

14. See D&C 90:24.

15. See D&C 6:20.

Photo Credits

page 2   Photograph © by Getty Images, Tao Associates.

page 10   Photograph © Jupiter Images Unlimited.

page 13   Photograph © Shutterstock Images,
photographer Jason Vandehey.

page 16   Photograph © Shutterstock Images,
photographer Marcel Mooij.

page 22   Photograph © Jupiter Images Unlimited.

pages 26–27   Photograph © Jupiter Images Unlimited.

pages 34–35   Photograph © Shutterstock Images,
photographer Alexander Raths.

pages 42–43   Photograph © Shutterstock Images,
photographer Kacso Sandor.

page 48   Photograph © Jupiter Images Unlimited.

About the Author

President Dieter F. Uchtdorf has served as the Second Counselor in the First Presidency of The Church of Jesus Christ of Latter-day Saints since February 3, 2008. He was sustained as a member of the Quorum of the Twelve Apostles in October 2004. He became a General Authority in April 1994 and served as a member of the Presidency of the Seventy from August 2002 until his call to the Twelve.

Prior to his calling as a General Authority, President Uchtdorf was the senior vice president of flight operations and chief pilot of Lufthansa German Airlines.

President Uchtdorf was born in 1940 in what is now the Czech Republic. He grew up in Zwickau, Germany, where his family joined the Church in 1947. He and his wife, Harriet Reich Uchtdorf, are the parents of two children and have six grandchildren.